GW00802268

Susanna Wesley

A fascinating insight into the life of
the mother of John and Charles Wesley.

G M Best

ISBN 978-1-901084-94-8

Printed and published by
WOODSPRING RESOURCE CENTRE
22a Griffin Road, Clevedon, BS21 6HH
Tel: 01275 870219

For
THE NEW ROOM
John Wesley's Chapel, 36 The Horsefair, Bristol BS1 3JE

Samuel Annesley

Susanna Wesley

Samuel Wesley in a modern portrait.
Oil on board by Richard Douglas 1998

SUSANNA WESLEY

1

THE BELOVED DAUGHTER

For many years Susanna Wesley's fame rested on her being the mother of John and Charles Wesley and she was, in the words of one historian, a kind of 'Methodist Madonna'. It then became fashionable for a time to say that she brought up her children too harshly and to try and discover what psychological damage she had caused them. This was followed by feminists seizing on her as an early example of an independent-minded woman who was not afraid to stand up for herself and who encouraged female education. More recently historians have come to recognise her importance as a writer and she has been hailed as a woman of great spiritual insight. What lies behind all these versions is the story of a gifted, intelligent woman whose spiritual strength enabled her not only to cope with family circumstances that would have crushed most women but also to brilliantly communicate that faith to her children, to the people round her, and to later generations through her writings.

Susanna was born on 20 January 1669, the youngest and last surviving daughter of a prominent dissenting minister called Dr Samuel Annesley, the nephew of the Earl of Anglesey. He was a good humoured and highly gifted man who had studied at Oxford and become first a chaplain in the parliamentary navy and then vicar of a church in Kent. He had then lost office for disapproving of the execution of Charles I, which he described as 'horrid murder', and calling Cromwell a hypocrite. Restored to favour after Cromwell's death, he had become a popular Puritan minister at St Giles' Church, Cripplegate, in 1658. He gained a reputation for being a great teacher. One of his pupils was the great writer Daniel Defoe who later said this inspiring man had 'nothing in him that was little or mean'.Other contemporary sources stress his sincerity, humility, wisdom, piety, and cheerfulness. John Wesley was to include some of Annesley's sermons in his 'Christian Library' and there are echoes of his grandfather's thinking in his emphasis on living a holy life.

Seven years prior to Susanna's birth Annesley had been expelled from St Giles for his refusal to accept the doctrine and liturgy of the Church of England as it was defined following the restoration of Charles II. She therefore grew up with her father controlling a large eight-hundred strong congregation of Presbyterians at Spitalfields. The family home was frequently visited by all the prominent dissenters of the day, including the famous theologian Richard Baxter.Samuel Annesley had twenty-five children but how many survived infancy is unknown. So far research has uncovered the names of only two sons and seven daughters. Susanna was a child of his second wife, Mary, of whom we know virtually nothing. According to a book published by one of her sons-in-law, Mary was the daughter of John White, a Puritan lawyer who had become a Member of Parliament.

Mary is likely to have had a large role in educating Susanna and her influence on how Susanna was to bring up her own children was probably quite significant. The word 'Puritan' often carries with it connotations of unhappy austerity but this certainly was not the case in the Annesley household, which was a cheerful and happy place. Susanna grew up not seeing religion as life-denying but as 'the most agreeable and delightful thing in the world'. She learnt to balance fun with faith:

> 'When I was young and too much addicted to childish diversions..... [I made the rule] never to spend more time in any matter of mere recreation in one day than I spent in private religious duties'.

However, her father made her appreciate 'faith without morality.... is but downright hypocrisy' and she later told one of her own daughters:

> 'Religion is not to be confined to the church, or closet, nor exercised only in prayer and meditation. Everywhere we are in the presence of God, and every word and action is capable of morality.'

Samuel and Mary educated their daughters far beyond what was normal for women at that time. In later life she said she had been blessed by good teaching and 'good books and ingenious conversation' and by the 'good example' set by her parents. Her father had a magnificent library and she was incredibly well read for a woman of that era. He encouraged her to think for herself and challenge whatever she was not prepared to accept. He told her to give her studies what he called 'heart-room' and to regularly reflect on whether she was thinking and behaving in the way Christ would expect of her. As an adult she was to strongly commendself-examination to her own children: 'The mind of a Christian should be... always disposed to hear the still, small voice of God's Holy Spirit'. To one of her daughters she wrote:

> ''Tis not learning these things by rote, nor the saying a few prayers morning and evening, that will bring you to heaven; you must understand what you say, and you must practise what you know.'

Having encouraged Susanna to think independently and to obey her conscience, Annesley could not really object when she told him in 1682 that she wished to join the Church of England rather than remain a nonconformist. Her sister Elizabeth later echoed their father's tolerance: 'The image of Christ is the same lovely thing, whether formed in a Church or a meeting'. It is unfortunate that we have lost Susanna's account of what led her to this decision. She told her eldest son it was based on reflecting on the arguments of both sides 'as far as they had come to my knowledge'. It therefore stemmed either from her extensive reading or from hearing discussions among her father's visitors. At this time the moderate Anglican clergy, many of whom had Puritan backgrounds, were doing all they could to win over the hearts of the non-conformists. There was also, of course, an element of discomfort applied – in the autumn of 1662 Annesley had his house broken into and some possessions confiscated because of his nonconformity.

It is just possible that romance strengthened Susanna's choice. In August 1682 at her sister Elizabeth's wedding she met for the first time the man who was to become her future husband, Samuel Wesley and he, not long afterwards, also announced he was abandoning dissent. Samuel was seven years her senior and had recently moved to London to study at a dissenting academy. Like her, he took religion very seriously because both his paternal grandfather and his father had been clergymen. The former had been a Puritan minister in Dorset while the latter had died when Samuel was very young, having been imprisoned four times for refusing to accept the 1662 Act of Uniformity. The ambitious Samuel immediately saw in Susanna an ideal prospective wife. She combined beauty and brains and was well connected. The thirteen-year old Susanna was flattered by his attentions, admiring his combination of affable wit and seriousness.

Samuel's departure from nonconformity opened the door for him to go to university. In 1684 he commenced studying at Exeter College, Oxford, with the express intention of seeking ordination. At some stage Annesley gave his consent for him to marry Susanna and their marriage took place on 11 November 1688. It thus coincided with the 'Glorious Revolution' of 1688-9 in which the Catholic James II was deposed in favour of his Protestant daughter Mary and her Dutch husband, William of Orange. Samuel approved of this, not least because as an undergraduate he had personally witnessed James II's autocratic manner during a royal visit to Oxford. However, Susanna thought it wrong to dethrone a God-anointed King. It was the first indicator that husband and wife were not perfectly matched in their views. In later years Susanna was sadly to confess to one of her children: 'Tis an unhappiness almost peculiar to our family that your father and I seldom think alike.' It cannot have helped that Samuel proved far more autocratic than her father and expected her to address him as 'Sir' and 'Master'.

Samuel was ordained on 24 February 1689 by the Bishop of London. His first clerical appointment was as a curate at St Botolph's, Aldersgate, but he and Susanna could not live on the tiny income this provided so he soon accepted a more lucrative post as a chaplain aboard a man-of-war in the Irish Sea. He said no hardship would make him ever repent his marriage. Susanna returned to live with her father and then discovered she was pregnant. She gave birth to a son on 10 February 1690 and he was named Samuel after his father and grandfather. Her husband returned to take up another post as a curate, this time at Newington Butts in Surrey. He tried to supplement an inadequate salary by writing articles on religious topics. It must have come as a great relief when a connection of the Annesleys, the Marquis of Normanby, enabled Samuel to obtain his first living in October 1691 and he thus became Vicar of South Ormsby, a small village of between two and three hundred people about twenty-five miles east of the cathedral city of Lincoln.

Moving from the world they knew to rural Lincolnshire was difficult for both of them. Samuel in particular hated the isolation and he dismissed his new home as just 'a mean cot, composed of reeds and clay'. It did not help that their infant son seemed unable to talk and that over her next three pregnancies Susanna lost one baby girl and two boy twins with only one daughter surviving. She was baptised Emilia in January 1693. The strain of being constantly pregnant was made worse for Susanna by her developing 'three or four touches of rheumatism', presumably because of the damp conditions within their home. Their financial situation was still dire and Samuel had to take on additional curacy work in the parish of South Thoresby. He spent what spare time he had writing verse, trying in vain to gain royal patronage by dedicating poetry to the Queen. The only good event was that their son Samuel's silence suddenly ended. According to family tradition he first spoke when he was aged five and under a table playing with his favourite cat. He heard Susanna anxiously looking for him and called out 'Here I am, mother'.

In one of the verses written at this time Samuel provides an insight into his relationship with his wife. He describes her as blessing his life because it was her 'pleasure to obey' and he bore 'an undisputed sway'. He felt he could treat any of her requests as 'commands' because they were always reasonable ones and she always 'studied my convenience and delight'. In fact Susanna was not as happy as he thought. She appreciated his piety and moral courage but was concerned at his constant search for promotion and his inability to be politic. The latter failing was shown to the full in 1695 when Samuel took exception that the mistress of a man renting the Marquis' house should dare to call on his wife. He ordered her out of his house, leaving her in no doubt about her immoral lifestyle. As a consequence he lost his post. Fortunately the Marquis of Normanby was prepared to find him another appointment – this time as Rector of St. Andrew's Church in Epworth, a small farming parish in north-west Lincolnshire.

This was deemed to be a very good post because it was worth potentially £150 to £200 per year, but Samuel did not see it in that light. He would have to turn part-time farmer to obtain this income and geographically Epworth was worse than South Ormsby. It was so remote there was not even a road within a forty-mile radius of it. Every winter it was reduced to being an island surrounded by fenland. Samuel delayed taking up the appointment till 1697, undertaking some work as a curate again. How could he go to Epworth knowing no one of any social worth ever went near it and his chance of gaining any prominence in the Church would be lost forever? As the months passed the extent of his borrowing became dangerously high. It is possible he hoped Susanna might inherit some money to offset this because her father was ill. If so, he was sadly disappointed. Annesley died in 1696 but left Susanna his books and papers rather than money. His real legacy was spiritual. According to John Wesley his mother said many times:

> 'She had been as sensible of the presence of the spirit of my grandfather as she could have been if she had seen him standing before her face'.

The mounting debt finally forced Samuel to move into the wilderness that was Epworth. His heart would have been even heavier had he known it was to be his and Susanna's home for the next thirty-nine years.

❑ ❑ ❑ ❑ ❑

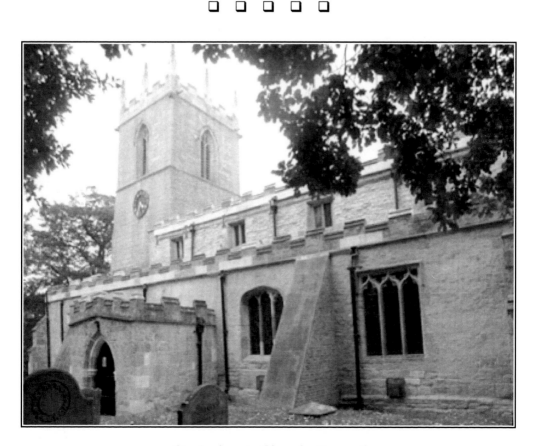

St. Andrew's Church, Epworth

2.

THE FAITHFUL WIFE

When Samuel Wesley became Rector of Epworth he estimated less than one in twenty of those in his parish could recite the Lord's Prayer and fewer the Creed. Only about twenty individuals regularly attended church services. His response was to try and visit all his parishioners and to offer two services every Sunday, mid-week prayers on Wednesdays and Fridays, and monthly communion services (at a time when the norm in rural areas was only about three or four times a year). He also ordered books and tracts from the newly created Society for the Promotion of Christian Knowledge and encouraged eight of the more receptive of his parishioners to form themselves into a London-style religious society to study the Bible. However, all this was in vain because the local people did not like his aloof manner, his High Anglican approach to worship, and his almost Puritanical dedication to church discipline.

His mounting frustration inevitably put strains on his marriage. Before going to Epworth he had viewed Susanna as a model of modesty and restraint, who 'graced my humble roof, and blest my life'. Now he increasingly saw her and their ever-increasing number of children as what was trapping him in a place he hated. By 1702, in addition to Samuel and Emila, there were Susanna (born 1695 and nicknamed Sukey), Mary (born 1696 and nicknamed Molly), Mehetebel (born 1697 and nicknamed Hetty), and Ann (born 1701 and nicknamed Nancy). Susanna had also given birth to three others who had died and her health had considerably suffered. Indicative of Samuel's feelings was his later advice to his son Samuel that he should 'burn romances', 'shut his eyes and heart against any sexual urges', and never marry if he wanted to become a great man. Susanna must have found his increasingly depressed state difficult, but she understood the cause:

> 'I should think it a thousand pities that a man of his brightness, and rare endowments of learning and useful knowledge, in relation to the church of God, should be confined to an obscure corner of the country, where his talents are buried.'

Matters came to a head over a relatively trivial action on her part. She had never really recognised the validity of deposing James II in 1688 and, after his daughter, Queen Anne, died in 1701, she saw even less reason to accept Anne's Dutch husband, William of Orange, as king. She therefore did not say 'Amen' when Samuel prayed for him. He demanded she should and she told him it was against her conscience. He then told her: 'You and I must part; for if we have two kings, we must have two beds'. He called down a curse on himself and their children if he ever touched her again until she had apologised to him and God. The normally submissive Susanna refused on the grounds he could not expect her to say something that ran counter to her conscience. Samuel dismissed this as pride and obstinacy. Although William of Orange was shortly afterwards killed in a riding accident, Samuel would not let the matter drop and said it was his intention to accuse her of treason to the church authorities. On 5 April he left Epworth, saying he would return to being a naval chaplain.

The deserted Susanna wrote for advice to Lady Yarborough, a noblewoman who was known to support the restoration of James II, saying:

> 'Since I am willing to let him quietly enjoy his opinions, he ought not to deprive me of my little liberty of conscience.'

She confessed she and Samuel were 'not likely to live happily together' but that with six very little children she was prepared to 'submit to anything or do anything in the world.... [except]'mock almighty God by begging pardon for what I think no sin'. Lady Yarborough advised her to seek the advice of Dr George Hickes, the Suffragan Bishop of Thetford, who had himself suffered for not swearing loyalty to the King. Susanna duly obliged and Hickes told her to 'stick to God and your conscience which are your best friends'.

When Samuel paid a final visit to see if Susanna would submit, she told him Hickes thought he could not expect her to perjure herself by making statements that ran contrary to her beliefs. He cursed her and walked out of the house, saying he intended to leave her forever. According to Susanna, she was saved from desertion only by the intervention of a neighbouring clergyman, who 'prevailed with him to return'. This was fortunate because a major fire shortly afterwards destroyed two-thirds of the Rectory. Some historians have surmised it was arson by a disaffected parishioner although Susanna thought it was the product of a careless accident by a servant. Both she and Samuel interpreted it as God's judgement on their quarrel and talk of him leaving the family was dropped. The immediate fruit of their reunion was the birth of John Wesley nine months later on 17 June 1703.

Samuel remained determined that neither he nor his sons' future should lie in Epworth. Although he could not afford the cost, he spent as much time as he could away in London and sent his elder son to Westminster School in 1704. His absences did little to endear him to his parishioners and in 1705 he also succeeded in offending some key local figures by supporting the wrong candidates in a parliamentary election. As a result he and his family faced a screaming mob that fired guns at the house. Susanna had only recently given birth again and the family nurse was so frightened she inadvertently smothered the child. Samuel wrote of this:

> '[They] ran up with it to my wife; and before she was well awake, threw it cold and dead into hers. She composed herself as well as she could, and that day got it buried'.

Samuel's enemies did not relent. They demanded that he pay money he owed, knowing he could not do so. This led to his immediate arrest and imprisonment in Lincoln Castle. He had been in considerable debt even before taking up his post at Epworth and he had borrowed more, first to provide furniture and the like for the rectory, then to repair the house after the fire of 1702, and finally to fund his visits to London and his son's school fees. His failure to run his farmland properly and collect tithes from hostile parishioners had not helped matters. Susanna offered to sell her rings (which were her only possessions) to make sure he was treated reasonably in prison, but he declined and bore his imprisonment with fortitude. He commenced writing a book on the story of Job - an apt topic for a man in his position.

It cannot have been easy for Susanna, who had been brought up in a relative affluent family, to cope with poverty and be left literally to fend for her family. One of her daughters later bemoaned Samuel's financial ineptitude that caused 'we of the female part of the family…. to get our own bread or starve.'. Susanna ensured her children were fed but was less careful about what she ate to the further detriment of her health. She sought help from the Archbishop of York:

> 'Strictly speaking, I never did want bread…. but then I have had so much care to get it before 'twas eat, and to pay for it after, as has often made it very unpleasant to me'.

She also sought assistance from her brother Samuel Annesley, who was a successful merchant, and her brother-in-law, Matthew Wesley, who was a London surgeon and apothecary. What assistance they gave was rather begrudging because her brother was critical of her husband's financial incompetence and her brother-in-law did not see why he should help bale out a large family when this was a product of Samuel's 'folly or vanity or ungovernable appetite'.

The problems were not just financial. The animosity felt towards Samuel was such that, even when he was in prison, someone attacked their housedog and their cows with a scythe. Susanna's continued loyalty owed much to her sense of duty. She had made her wedding vows before God and her father had taught her: 'Consult duty not events. There is nothing in the world for us to do, but to mind our duty'. Unfortunately the only duty Samuel performed, once he was released from prison, was to continue making his wife pregnant. She suffered further miscarriages and infant deaths, but still managed to add three more children to the family, bringing the total to ten. These were Martha (born 1706 and nicknamed Patty), Charles (born 1707) and Kezzia (born 1710 and nicknamed Kezzy). Susanna's response to having this many children from an estimated nineteen pregnancies was: 'It is no small honour to be entrusted with the care of so many souls'.

Samuel made no effort to resolve his debts. He continued to regularly visit London, ever hopeful that one day his talents would be recognized. Susanna may have been thinking of this when she wrote on one occasion in her Journal:

> *'Those persons that are uneasy to themselves can never be easy to those about them'.*

Local opposition continued to grow and it was during one of Samuel's visits home in 1709 that the Epworth Rectory once again caught on fire. The blaze started in the middle of the night and it may have been an arson attack. Susanna, who was almost eight months pregnant at the time, afterwards wrote how the family had no time to don clothes and ran naked out of their burning home. Her legs and face were burnt when three times she ran back into the flames to rescue her family. All the children were safely got out except for the six-year old John who was trapped upstairs in a bedroom. Fortunately a resourceful parishioner told another to climb on his shoulders and so reach him. John was snatched to safety literally minutes before the burning thatch roof collapsed into the room. The whole family felt their escape was miraculous, but especially that of John, who was described as 'a brand plucked from the burning'.

The house and its contents and all their personal belongings were totally destroyed and rebuilding their home was to lead to real hardship for many years, even though the Ecclesiastical Commissioners paid part of the cost. Despite this, Samuel still insisted on continuing his costly visits to London, on funding his elder son through Oxford, and on sending his other sons, John and Charles, to Charterhouse School and Westminster School in 1714 and 1716 respectively. One of his daughters later recalled the outcome:

> *'For seven winters my father was in London, and we at home in intolerable want and affliction... vast income but no comfort or credit from it.'*

Susanna found it hard that the family's finances remained so poor despite all her efforts to save money by 'care, frugality, and industry', but she tried to hide the full impact from Samuel:

'I conceal our wants from him as much as possible, lest he should be afflicted beyond measure and because I know that if he were acquainted with each particular, he would…. borrow [more] money rather than I or his children should be distressed'.

She never expressed any self-pity or bitterness at her hard and difficult lifestyle or her frequent ill-health, even though at one stage she found it necessary to write in her private Journal that she should guard against resorting to drinking too much alcohol. She remained convinced that whatever happened was God's will and her faith would see her through saying to herself: 'Rest assured that all things shall at last have a happy issue if the heart be but sincerely devoted to God'. She turned her running of the family home into her service to God. The nearest to a complaint is the following comment in a letter to her eldest son:

Samuel and Susanna Wesley
A modern reconstruction from
contemporary portraits by
Richard Douglas

'I have constantly enough pain enough to mind me of mortality and trouble enough in my circumstances of fortune to exercise my patience'.

In 1721 her brother urged her to consider leaving a husband who had so conspicuously failed to provide properly for his family and who had not even paid off the money he had borrowed for clothes and furniture thirteen years earlier. In reply she made clear the reasons for her continued loyalty to Samuel:

'I am… infirm and weak….. [but] old as I am, since I have taken my husband for better or worse, I'll make my residence with him. Where he lives will I live and where he dies will I die and there will I be buried. God do so to me and more also, if ought but death part him and me.'

If there was a downside to all this it was that her son John was later to voice how hard he found it to contemplate marriage with anyone because he did not believe he could ever find 'such a woman as my father had'.

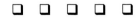

3.

THE LOVING MOTHER

To a certain extent Susanna and Samuel learnt to live separately. His domain was his study and the church, hers the kitchen and bringing up the children. Susanna summed up her approach to motherhood by saying:

'I do not love distance or ceremony; there is more of love and tenderness in the name of mother than in all the complimental titles in the world'.

Her love for her children springs out repeatedly in her writing and is equally evidenced in what they had to say about her. For example, she told her eldest son, Samuel, 'I love you as my own soul', and he called her 'the best of mothers'. When he left home to study at Westminster School, she wrote regularly to him, expressing her love and, lest schoolmates lead him astray, reminding him of the need to work hard so he could 'surpass all others in virtue and learning'. Some of her letters have survived because, on her advice, he copied them into a book to which he could refer. Their contents are dominated by a deep desire that he understand the importance of putting spiritual matters first:

'In all things endeavour to act upon principle, and do not live like the rest of mankind, who pass through the world like straws upon a river, which are carried which way the stream or wind drives them.'

She made clear to Samuel that what God was interested in was people's intentions rather than judging them on what they managed to achieve: 'Our sincere endeavours to do our duty shall be accepted though we fail in the performance'. However, it was vital to 'go as far as we can and love him to the utmost of our capacity'. Looking for support to the Holy Spirit would transform good intentions into 'a constant and steady course of virtue'. Reading and studying the Bible was essential so that a person would grasp what direction God wanted their life to take. Caring for others was equally essential because 'we express our love to God by being friendly and beneficent to all that bear his image.'

She told him to avoid 'ignorance, error, unbelief, misbelieve and disbelief' and to always remember the fallen nature of mankind: 'Take care of the world, lest it unawares steal away your heart'. Susanna especially warned Samuel against excessive drinking, which would take away his judgement and lead him into bad behaviour: 'Stay at the third glass – one for thirst and one for refreshment is sufficient'. He was never to do anything wrong simply because of peer pressure from friends because 'the ways of virtue are infinitely better than the practice of vice':

> *'Remember how short and how uncertain this life is! And what depends upon it! Make a stand! Recollect your thoughts! Think again upon eternity!..... Man is not to be depended upon. God is all in all. Those whom he blesses shall be blest indeed!'*

Elsewhere she added:

> *'Pause and say to yourself, 'What am I about to do?' God sees me! Is this my avowed faithfulness to my Creator, Redeemer, and Sanctifier?'*

In view of the later creation of Methodism, it is interesting to see how much Susanna promoted the idea of developing a methodical daily routine to improve one's faith:

> *'Throw all your business into a certain method, by which means you'll learn to improve every precious moment.... Begin and end the day with him who is Alpha and Omega... [and] assign what time you should spend in private devotion.... Appoint so much time for sleep, eating, company, etc....[and] be very nice in the choice of your company.'*

Susanna took pride in the fact Samuel won himself a scholarship and became the protégé of the Dean of Westminster, Francis Atterbury. How to bring out the best in the rest of her children became increasingly the focus of her attention after the 1709 fire. For months all but Emily had to stay with neighbours and Susanna bemoaned that this experience corrupted them:

> *'In those [homes] they were left at full liberty to converse with servants.... and to run abroad to play with any children, good or bad. They soon learned to neglect a strict observance of the Sabbath; and got knowledge of several songs and bad things.... [Their] civil behavior ....was in a great measure lost and a clownish accent and many rude ways were learnt'.*

She vowed on their return to the rebuilt Rectory:

> *'There is nothing I now desire to live for but to do some small service to my children; that as I have brought them into the world, I may, if it please God, be an instrument of doing good to their souls'.*

Both Puritan and Anglican circles had long promoted the important role of a mother in educating children and Susanna reminded herself in her journal of the famous lines from Proverbs: 'Train up a child in the way he should go, and when he is old he will not depart from it'. Her reading of the works of the philosopher John Locke had reinforced the importance of being firm with children and making them respect parental authority. Given her own education, she treated her daughters' education as being just as essential as that of her sons, decrying those mothers who gave sewing priority over reading for their girls. After Kezzia's birth in 1710, she had more time to systematize her educational role because she ceased to be of childbearing age.

For the first year of each child's life she endeavoured to get it into a routine in term of its sleeping, eating, and dressing and undressing habits. Once the child was a year old it was taught to 'cry softly' so as not to disturb Samuel and the household in order to escape 'abundance of correction'. Susanna held that smacking a child when small avoided the necessity of more severe physical punishment as they got older. Then only 'a finger held up was sufficient to restrain or correct'. Any form of physical punishment does not fit comfortably with some of today's child-rearing philosophies and a few writers have implied she wrecked her children's lives by crushing their wills so that even as mature adults they found it difficult to do anything but obey her. This is nonsense. Susanna actively encouraged independent thinking and therefore did not want to crush her children's spirit, merely their selfishness. If as adults they liked to please her that was because they loved her not because they feared her. Susanna never approved of any punishment without due cause or appropriate restraint, and she thought praise was essential, saying every act of obedience 'should be always commended and frequently rewarded'.

The allegation of harshness also ignores that Susanna clearly believed parents should make allowances for their children because of 'the weakness of their reason, and immaturity of their judgements'. She was adept at turning a blind eye, accepting that 'a great many childish follies and inadvertencies may be passed by'. She never punished a child for doing something wrong if the intention was good. She was always very ready to forgive. It was her rule never to bring up past offences because 'no child should ever be chid or beat twice for the same fault'. Most important of all, Susanna held there was no need for any punishment if a child confessed his or her guilt and promised to amend. Charles Wesley reflected her views in one of his hymns on bringing up children:

> 'We would persuade their hearts to obey;
> With mildest zeal proceed;
> And never take the harsher way
> When love will do the deed.'

Susanna thought parents who laid great store on being 'kind and indulgent' were simply enabling their child to grow up 'headstrong' and 'wilful':

> 'Self-will is the root of all sin and misery, so whatever cherishes this in children insures... [their] wretchedness and irreligion; whatever checks and mortifies it promotes their future happiness and piety... Religion is nothing else than doing the will of God, and not our own... The parent, who studies to subdue self-will in his child, works together with God in the renewing and saving a soul. The parent who indulges it does the devil's work; makes religion impracticable [and] salvation unattainable.'

In a treatise on education John Wesley was to echo her views, saying it was a parent's role 'to correct with kind severity' rather than see a child become ill-disciplined.

Early obedience and good behaviour were at the core of her children's upbringing. They were never given anything in response to them crying or making a fuss. If they spoke to anyone they had to do so politely and remember when appropriate to say 'please' and 'thank you'. They had to seek permission before doing anything, even leaving the room. There was a strict ban on swearing or using any obscenities or being rude in any way. When the family sat down together for three set meals a day, they were expected to observe proper table manners. No one was permitted to shout for what they wanted at table. They had to make whispered requests instead. They also had to eat what they were given and they were not permitted to have any snacks between meals. There were strict bedtimes. If sick, they had to take medicine without complaint. When they played they had to do so quietly so as not to disturb others and Susanna monitored with whom her children socially mixed. Bedtime was strictly enforced and there was never any sitting by a child till it fell asleep. All this may sound draconian but the children looked back on their childhood with affection because underlying the regime was their mother's unquestioned love.

Susanna usually waited till a child was five before embarking on their formal education. Prior to that age she contented herself with teaching them only a few basic things, such as being able to recite the Lord's Prayer and a few collects and passages from Scripture. Once they were five, they were expected to study with her for six hours a day. The only child who ever had an outside tutor was Samuel. There was no money to pay for the others. No excuses were accepted and no play was permitted during lesson time, only 'vigorous application'. At the end of each morning and each afternoon each child had to tell her what they had learnt. She appears to have been a charismatic teacher because her children later spoke with affection of how happily and quickly the time in their lessons passed. Part of her success lay in her incredible patience. On one occasion Samuel was amazed to hear his wife go over a topic twenty times with one of the children and he told her he could not understand how she could do that. She replied: '

> If I had satisfied myself by mentioning it only nineteen times, I should have lost all my labour. It was the twentieth time that crowned it.'

In many families there are problems because of the rivalry between siblings. The Wesley house was not immune from that but Susanna tried to minimise the danger of this developing. She did not allow any child 'to invade the property of another in the smallest matter, though it were but of the value of a farthing or a pin'. No one could borrow anything without seeking its owner's permission. If one of them was given a gift, it was his or her sole right to decide what to do with it. Naturally the older children were also expected to help with the younger ones. Susanna also made sure that she gave each of her children her undivided attention for a period of time on a given day each week. In this way she showed that each of them mattered to her and made sure she could meet their individual needs. And, of course, each child's best behaviour was encouraged by the constant daily religious routine of prayers, psalm-singing, and Bible reading.

The Epworth rectory was a happy place, despite all the hardships the family faced. Contrary to the image that people have of those who come from a Puritan background, there was, amid the seriousness, also lots of laughter and time for games, including even the playing of cards. John Wesley recognised the importance of her even-handed approach, saying it was important to let children see that religion was not 'an austere, melancholy thing'. Her approach to her children's education not only laid the foundations for him and Charles to follow their brother Samuel to school and university but also made them appreciate the educational importance of uniting, in the words of Charles, 'knowledge' with 'vital piety'. John told the teachers at Kingswood School to remember 'an ounce of love was worth a pound of knowledge' and embodied her educational system in a treatise written for parents. This included telling them they should never treat their children like parrots, who learnt only by repeating what they did not understand.

❑   ❑   ❑   ❑   ❑

The back kitchen at the Epworth Rectory today, laid out as a schoolroom

4

PREACHER OF RIGHTEOUSNESS

Susanna's grasp of the religious debates taking place in the eighteenth century is very evident in an imagined dialogue that she wrote between her and her daughter Emily on 'the being and attributes of God' and 'the principles of revealed religion'. It ranges from the ideas of Aristotle, Plato and other ancient Greeks to the writings of the scientist Robert Boyle, various Anglican theologians, and philosophers like Pascal, Malebranche, and Locke. For a woman in the eighteenth-century it is a remarkable piece of writing, especially as she was not afraid to 'beg to differ' with their arguments. Here one sees why John Wesley was to argue so strongly for a rational Christianity, one unafraid of tackling difficult questions.

However, Susanna's faith was just as much about the heart as the head. In her Journal she warned herself against becoming too intellectual in her approach to her faith:

'Submit your reason so far to your faith as not to doubt or scruple those points of faith which are mysterious to us through the weakness of our understanding, and adore the mystery you cannot comprehend. Be not too curious in prying into those secret things that are known only to God'.

This acceptance of the mysterious was to feature prominently in many of the hymns of her son Charles Wesley. Susanna never believed a person could rely on reason alone to define what to believe: 'God only knows what God is....Finite can never comprehend infinite'.

Susanna withdrew for private devotion for an hour every morning and every evening and for a shorter time at noon and this provided her with the strength to face whatever the day brought. She said her ideal life would have been one of reflection had not she owed duties to her husband and children. The journal of her daily spiritual reflections is often memorable and many extracts have now been adapted into prayers for publication. No wonder she wrote:

'If to esteem and have the highest reverence for thee.... if earnestly and constantly to desire thee, thy favour, thy acceptance.... if to feel a vital joy overspread and cheer the heart at each perception of thy blessedness.... be to love thee – I do love thee!'

Susanna saw formal worship on a Sunday as a special time to refresh her soul. In an uncompleted exposition on the Ten Commandments she says the Sabbath day must be set aside for 'our nobler and better part' as the time when we offer 'our highest praises'. To those who argued they had better things to do on a Sunday she argued 'the mind will savour most and be most strongly affected with what it thinks most upon'. Not surprisingly, she chose to lead Sunday evening worship for her family whenever Samuel was away from home.In the winter of 1711 a servant asked if his parents could attend and then, in Susanna's words, 'others who heard of it begged leave also so our company increased to about thirty and seldom exceeded forty'. Family evening prayers thus became full evening services. Her nonconformist childhood probably made this seem acceptable even though it ran counter to what the Church permitted.

We do not know what sermons Susanna read out on these occasions, but we have hints in her Journal about her approach. She aimed to speak plainly because people like 'a simple, plain, unaffected honesty' and she believed the best prayers were not extempore ones but those given careful thought beforehand. She also thought it vital to preach only what she herself practised because people are 'more apt to observe what you do than what you say'.

The strength of her faith and her ease in communicating what she believed is evident in the personal version of the Apostle's Creed, which she dedicated to her daughter Sukey. It opens with a personal statement:

> 'I do truly and heartily assent to the being of a God, one supreme independent power, who is a spirit, infinitely wise, holy, good, just, true, unchangeable'.

Then it examines God's 'boundless, incomprehensible, and eternal' nature as 'the great parent of the universe', before moving onto her favourite topic, the importance of Jesus. She saw the virgin birth as a natural consequence of the mysterious nature of God made man, something 'altogether differing from ordinary generations'. His suffering, though 'from eternity decreed' in order to save sinful mankind, was no less real – the persecution by Herod that made him a refugee as a child, the role of carpenter that made him 'despicable [and] of no reputation', the severity of forty days in the wilderness, the constant 'painful travelling from place to place', and, above all, the rejection of his love. And when she reaches the crucifixion she suddenly moves from talking of the past to making the reader live the scene:

> 'See him retire to a solitary garden at a still, melancholy hour of night; behold him prostrate on the ground..... See with what cruel pleasure they nail his hands and feet to the infamous wood'.

She dwells not just on the physical torment but the spiritual agony of bearing the sins of the world before moving onto his resurrection and ascension and a future day of judgement.

For those who questioned life after death, she has a clear reply: 'omnipotence knows no difficulty'. In our resurrected bodies we shall have our understanding of God 'illuminated' and 'enlarged' so that we can 'fully comprehend the divine nature' and nevermore be troubled with 'misapprehensions or false conceptions of him'. Whilst recognising the existence of Hell, Susanna waxes lyrical only on Heaven, that wonderful place where there will be 'no unruly passions', 'no pain and misery', and 'no more death, neither sorrow, nor crying'. Until that place was reached she relied on being part of 'the communion of saints':

> 'We join with all the company of the heavenly host in praying and admiring the Supreme Being.... all members of the same mystical body of Christ.... and though we are not actually possessed of the happiness they enjoy [in Heaven], yet we have the Holy Spirit given us as an earnest of our eternal felicity with them hereafter'.

In 1712 Susanna read a book about Danish missionaries in India and it inspired her to evangelise more:

> 'At present it came into my mind, though I am not a man nor a minister of the gospel, and so cannot be employed in such a worthy employment as they were, yet if my heart were sincerely devoted to God, and if I were inspired with a true zeal for his glory and really did desire the salvation of souls, I might do somewhat more than I do'.

The result was that, when Samuel was again absent in the winter months, she allowed the number attending her Sunday evening service to rise to over two hundred. She says she 'discoursed more freely and affectionately than before' and 'chose the best and most awakening sermons' to read. This inevitably drew the wrath of the curate that Samuel had appointed to undertake his parish responsibilities, not least because he could hardly attract any congregation at all! He complained to Samuel, who immediately ordered Susanna to stop because he felt no woman should be undertaking priestly functions. A righteously indignant Susanna stuck to her guns:

> 'In your absence I cannot but look upon every soul you leave under my care as a talent committed to me under a trust by the great lord of all the families of heaven and earth'.

She told him all around her she saw the good consequences of what she was doing. Families were now attending church that had never done so before. The terrible hostility of the parishioners to the Wesley family was being replaced by the 'the greatest amity'. She would only stop if he took full responsibility for any souls that might be damned as a consequence of her inaction. Samuel dropped his opposition and the services continued.

Both Charles and John Wesley were to recall their mother's refusal to give up her preaching when they subsequently used lay preachers despite opposition from clergy. In his later years John was even to turn a blind eye to some of his female followers engaging in leading worship. Had not his mother been 'a preacher of righteousness' and did not the saving of souls outweigh all else? However, it would be wrong to see Susanna as a pioneering feminist. Though she defied Samuel and convention in leading worship because her faith demanded it, her normal stance was to accept the position of women in society as God's will. She never stopped describing Samuel as her 'Master' and time and again in her Journal she reminds herself that the key qualities required of her are 'submission and resignation'.

Given Susanna's impressively rational examination of her faith, scholars have expressed surprise at her acceptance that the Rectory was haunted and the story of 'Old Jeffrey' has therefore become something of a cause celebre. On 2 December 1716 one of the family's servants heard knockings on the door when no one was there and, when he retired to bed, saw a strange object whirling to the accompaniment of sounds which were similar to a gobbling turkey-cock. The next day a maid heard knockings in the dairy and then it was the turn of Molly and Sukey Wesley to hear strange sounds. Susanna thought it was just their imagination, but then she heard the sound of a rocking cradle in a room where there was none. On one occasion her oldest daughter Emily reported she heard noises and, when Susanna looked under her bed, 'something ran out pretty much like a badger'. Samuel told the whole family not to be silly, but was taken aback when he heard the knocking by his bedside. Bottles kept under the stairs were found smashed, wood was mysteriously planed, and the jack in the kitchen used to roast meat was repeatedly wound up. The apparently supernatural sounds and activities continued frequently and usually in the evenings until the end of January 1717 but after that only sounds were heard and those extremely rarely.

Writing to her son Samuel, Susanna told him she had sought to explain away the noises by arguing it must be 'only rats or weasels that disturbed us', but in the end she had had to admit 'that it was beyond the power of any human creature to make such strange and various noises' because all the family had been present on occasions when the knocking was heard. Susanna called it 'the unwelcome guest' but Emily began nicknaming it 'Old Jeffrey'. Historians have tended to see the strange events as a practical joke engineered either by a servant or, far more probably, by one of the family themselves, possibly Hetty, who was the most mischievous of the Wesley children. However, because John Wesley talked about 'Old Jeffrey' the case later became well known and opponents of Methodism seized on it as proof that the movement was irrationally fanatical. It was a pity he did not heed Susanna's advice on the issue: 'I would not have the matter imparted to any'. There were far greater and far more important mysteries to explore than that of inexplicable sounds.

5

THE DISTRESSED PARENT

Unhappy romances and marriages seemed to beset Susanna's daughters in the 1720s and 1730s and this caused her much distress. Her eldest daughter, Emilia (known as Emily) was attractive in appearance and lively in personality, and she was invited to stay with her uncle Matthew Wesley in London in the hope she could find work as a governess. There she fell in love with Robert Leybourne, a highly educated friend of her brother John. Unfortunately she had to return to Epworth because no employment came her way. She kept in contact with Leybourne for three years until Susanna ordered her to desist (largely on the advice of her son Samuel who presumably thought Leybourne would have married her if his intentions had been serious). For years Susanna then had to cope with a daughter who spoke of death as 'a consummation devoutly to be wished'. The once amenable Emily became bitter, vowed never to marry, and sought a career as a teacher in Lincoln. In 1731 Matthew Wesley enabled her to create her own school in Gainsborough. There she entered into a relationship with a doctor who was a Quaker. This came to an abrupt end after an argument, primarily because Emily heeded to her brother John, who opposed her marrying a nonconformist. Possibly on the rebound Emily married an apothecary called Robert Harpur in 1735. He proved a wastrel who reduced her to dire poverty and their one child died in infancy.

A similar disaster befell the vivacious and good-natured second daughter Sukey. After the 1709 fire she and her sister Hetty also went to London to stay with Matthew Wesley. Both then found returning to Epworth very difficult. Hetty described it as a place 'debarred of wisdom, wit, and grace' and its inhabitants as 'asses dull, on dunghills born… a sordid race'. Sukey was quick to take up an offer to return to London and stay with her other uncle, Samuel Annesley. There she met a relatively wealthy landowner called Richard Ellison and in 1719 she married him without seeking parental permission. It was a disastrous mistake. The little information we have indicates he proved to be 'common, coarse and uncultivated'. He treated Sukey harshly and despotically, sometimes physically abusing her. Susanna said her daughter had married an irreligious man 'little inferior to the apostate angels in wickedness', but she encouraged Sukey to accept her unhappy lot, especially as the couple had four children. Matters got worse after 1735 when a series of events destroyed Ellison's wealth. It is surmised that the final straw that forced Sukey to leave him was his setting fire to their home, presumably whilst drunk.

An even worse fate befell Hetty, probably the most intelligent, witty and gifted of Susanna's daughters. She was distressed at her father's 'sour-faced' attitude to any of her suitors. She pinned her hopes on marrying a handsome graduate called John Romley, who had been appointed as her father's curate when Samuel acquired the parish of Wroote to add to that of Epworth. Unfortunately Samuel overheard Romley singing a popular song which he deemed vulgar and so he dismissed him and banned him from the house. Hetty tried to secretly communicate with Romley so Samuel sent her away to serve as a governess to a family in the town of Kelstein. In March 1725 Hetty wrote to her brother John:

> 'I had far rather have gone to my grave!… I am in no great measure careless what becomes of me. Home I would not go to, were I reduced to beggary, and here I will never stay… I intend to try my hand in London… [Here] I am condemned to constant solitude.'

Trying her hand in London was her coded way of saying she had decided to elope with a local lawyer called Will Atkins. She felt driven to this by her father's rejection of Atkins as a worthy suitor for her. Unfortunately she had chosen the worst kind of man. She was forced to return home after only one disastrous night in which it became clear that sex rather than marriage was the lawyer's desire. Samuel refused to forgive her and, when he discovered she was pregnant, insisted on her immediately marrying another man as soon as he could find anyone prepared to have her. This proved to be a poorly educated and boorish glazier and plumber called William Wright from the nearby town of Louth. Only her crippled sister Mary had the courage to try to stop this, telling her father:

> 'You are seldom kind and rarely just… You are a tyrant to those you love; and now in your tyranny you are going to do… a downright wickedness'.

Hetty and Wright were married on 13 October 1725. It was a disastrous match made worse by her husband's tendency towards heavy drinking and physical abuse. In the circumstances it is not surprising that Hetty's child proved frail and only survived a couple of months.

Susanna initially shared her husband's harsh response to Hetty's misbehaviour but in the summer of 1726 she changed her attitude, having heard her son John urge forgiveness. She decided to visit her erring daughter, but found Hetty to be resentful, greeting her arrival 'without the least emotion of joy or grief' and listening to her 'with great indifference'. Hetty clearly felt that if anyone required pardon it was her parents rather than her. Susanna returned home feeling 'strangely mortified, neither pleased with her nor myself.'. Samuel simply took the line that John was defending immorality. It was left to Hetty's brother Samuel and her uncle Matthew to help her by setting up her husband with a business in London so she was no longer humiliated in Epworth. Her father never forgave her and it was only after his death that Susanna saw her daughter again. In between there were to be years of misery for Hetty, not least because all her subsequent children died, a fact she partially attributed to her father's refusal to pray for her.

It is thought Susanna's favourite daughter was Martha (known as 'Patty'), either because she was the most serious minded or because she looked very like her brother John. Charles Wesley commented that Patty was 'too wise to be witty'. In 1720 her uncle Matthew Wesley invited her to London and Susanna expressed her concern that she might allow herself to be courted by the wrong sort of man:

> 'Tis pity that honest, generous girl has not a little of the subtlety of the serpent with the innocence of the dove'.

In the event Patty had various suitors. Like Hetty before her, she was attracted to John Romley and her father put paid to that by sending her away for a time to be a governess. Eventually the man who attracted her most was Westley Hall, one of her brother John's tutees. They became secretly betrothed. However, this did not stop him courting her younger sister Kezzy, who knew nothing about his relationship with Patty, when he accompanied John on a visit to Epworth. In 1734 Hall gained the family's approval to marry Kezzy only to have an outraged Patty then force him to honour his original commitment to her. Charles Wesley felt Kezzy, who had long suffered from an inferiority complex, never recovered from the shock. Not surprisingly it was to prove another unhappy marriage, although Susanna was not to live to see the worst of it. In later years Westley Hall had a number of adulterous affairs and illegitimate children. Patty herself had ten children, though only one survived infancy.

History has judged that the only daughters to marry satisfactorily were Anne and Mary but even this is questionable. Anne or 'Nancy' was married to a well-educated land surveyor called John Lambert in December 1725. The couple appear to have been happy, but he increasingly developed a drink problem and their only son died at the age of about nine. In 1733 Mary (known as 'Molly') married John Whitelamb, a poor curate who had been virtually adopted by her father. Samuel handed over the living of Wroote to him so he could marry her. Susanna opposed the match, partly because she thought Molly's crippled body made marriage and childbirth a difficult prospect and partly because she thought Whitelamb unequal to her daughter's merits (not least because he had had an affair with another woman). Susanna prayed for 'God to bring good out of this great evil'. The marriage was never really tested because Molly died in childbirth in November 1734.

Samuel   *John*   *Charles*

While dealing with the various issues affecting her daughters, Susanna had to also cope with three other distressing family issues. The first was the collapse of her eldest son Samuel's career hopes in the 1720s. This was because he insisted on defending his patron and friend, Francis Atterbury, who had become Bishop of Rochester. Atterbury had refused to sign a declaration of loyalty during the abortive Jacobite Rebellionof 1715 and become a major critic of the government. In 1722 he was arrested for treason and sentenced to banishment. Samuel criticized the government and instantly lost all chance of becoming Headmaster of Westminster. He was eventually forced to leave London, becoming instead the Headmaster of the far inferior Blundell's School in Devon in 1732.

The second issue was the mysterious disappearance of her brother, Samuel Annesley. In 1724 Susanna took the unusual step of going to Oxford and London, probably in the hope of seeking assistance from her brother, who was due to return home after having spent over four years working in East India. However, when the ship docked he did not disembark to greet his waiting sister. Neither he nor his money was ever heard of again and it is now assumed he may have been murdered. This meant the family's financial situation continued to deteriorate. The little information we have all points to the conditions within the Epworth Rectory becoming ever more basic. Susanna's life became one of continuously scrimping and saving with no prospect of relief from any source.

The third issue was both her and her husband's declining health. By the early 1730s Susanna's hard lifestyle had taken its toll so that, as she told her son John, 'every member of the body is a seat of pain'. She was compelled to frequently spend much of her time confined to her room. In June 1731 the

69 year-old Samuel badly injured his head when he was flung out of a wagon whose horses had bolted. His health took a serious downturn and by 1733 he was begging his son John to leave Oxford and take over his duties at Epworth. He knew if that did not happen Susanna and those daughters still at home would be evicted when he died. John's selfish refusal to come to his parents' aid upset both of them but Susanna did not complain. She simply told John that everyone could see his father's 'decay'. Dealing with a dying husband put immense strains on her and, in the end, she had to largely hand over his care to her daughter Emily and son Charles. Samuel died 'full of faith and peace' on 25 April 1735. After 39 years the Rectory at Epworth could no longer be Susanna's home.

How did Susanna cope with all these distressing family circumstances? The best clue is contained in a letter written in 1727 to her son John:

> 'I often revolve the state of my family and the wants of my children over in my mind…. When I behold them struggling with misfortunes of various kinds, some without sufficiency of bread, in the most literal sense, all destitute of the conveniences or comforts of life, it puts me upon the expostulation of David, 'Lo, I have sinned and I have done wickedly, but these sheep, what have they done?' Though thus the tenderness of a mother pleads their cause, yet I dare not dispute God's justice, wisdom, or goodness'.

6.

MOTHER OF METHODISM

G iven the family problems occurring in the 1720s and 1730s, it is amazing that Susanna constantly devoted time to guiding the spiritual development of her two younger sons, John and Charles. Whatever her husband's limitations, Susanna remained proud of the fact he was 'a religious orthodox man' and she wanted her sons to follow suit. John went as a student to Christ Church, Oxford in 1720 and, after obtaining his degree, embarked on an M.A. In 1725 he was ordained and, shortly afterwards, became a tutor at Lincoln College. Charles went to Christ Church in 1726 and, after initially tasting student freedom, looked to John to guide his religious thinking. Throughout this time John and Susanna regularly exchanged letters and Charles was always keen to know what their mother thought about issues. A number of her letters have survived and, while they include family issues, their focus is theological discussion or what Susanna called 'practical divinity'. They show more than anything else why Susanna was critical to the creation of Methodism as we know it.

Initially her concern was that John would decide to abandon seeking a degree because of the inadequate funding provided by his family. She told him 'be not discouraged; do your duty; keep close to your studies, and hope for better days', and advised him not to be too bound up with the pleasure-seeking normally associated with student life:

> 'The beauty, ease, and pleasures of the world strongly charm us; the wealth and honours of the world allure us... [but this] utterly deprives us of our moral liberty and by consequence makes us wretched'.

She urged him to 'enter upon a serious examination' of himself and seek ordination. She believed in daily meditation and reflection, in regular prayer and Bible study, in undertaking good works. John undoubtedly copied her in keeping a daily journal and the methodical routines he eventually established were very much based on her recommendations. In her words, 'habits are got by repeated acts and cannot otherwise be acquired'.

In 1729 she welcomed Charles' decision to create the religious society that was later nicknamed 'the Holy Club'. She approved of John taking over its leadership and initially only questioned his excessive belief in mortifying the flesh through fasting. She feared this would endanger Charles' already frail health. As far as she was concerned 'fasting was helpful for most people but hurtful to some and unnecessary to others'. There were better ways of becoming virtuous. She was less impressed with what was happening when John became obsessed with earning his salvation. As early as 1725 she had been warning him people were saved only 'through the merits of our Redeemer'. In 1734 she reminded him 'no man can qualify himself for heaven' and told him to heed the advice of the theologian Richard Baxter:

> 'Put your souls, with all their sins and dangers….into the hand of Jesus Christ your Saviour; and trust them wholly with him by a resolved faith'.

John and Charles were not to appreciate this truth until their hearts were 'strangely warmed' in 1738. She thought their agonizing over their failure to live up to their faith unhelpful. She wrote to a friend:

> 'One reason why Christians are so often subject to despond is that they look more to themselves than to their Saviour; they would establish a righteousness of their own to rest on, without adverting enough to the sacrifice of Christ, by which alone we are justified before God'.

She said John was foolish to think he was a failure if he was not always conscious of God's presence:

> 'That God is everywhere present, and we always present to him, is certain; but that he should be always present to us is scarce consistent with our mortal state'.

She was delighted when in 1738 he and Charles stopped agonising and grasped 'that stupendous mercy offered us by redeeming love', but she thought it 'an odd way of thinking' for them to claim they had not therefore been Christians before. She told them they had 'saving faith' before but 'it is one thing to have faith, and another thing to be sensible we have it'.

What Susanna admired most was her sons' determination to serve God. That is not surprising because she had taught them the 'highest and most noble part of Christian life…. consists in loving God…. with the full power and energy of the soul'. John was later to define a Methodist as 'one who loves the Lord his God with all his heart, with all his soul, with all his mind, and with all his strength'. Charles was to write:

> 'Take my soul and body's powers
> Take my memory, mind and will
> All my goods, and all my hours
> All I know and all I feel
> All I think, or speak or do
> Take my heart, but make it new.'

For Susanna it was important that such love should be put ahead of doctrinal differences:

> 'Some truths... are of so little importance to the salvation of mankind.... that they ought not to be contended for, nor ever asserted at the expense of peace and charity. Let, therefore, the general bent of your mind and conversation tend to peace and unity'.

John later echoed this in his advice to Methodists:

> 'Every wise man ...[only asks]: 'Is thy heart right with God?....Is thy faith filled with the energy of love?.... Is thy heart right toward thy neighbour?'... If it be, give me thy hand. I do not mean, 'Be of my opinion'.... I do not mean, 'Embrace my modes of worship'.... Let these smaller points stand aside.... I mean....love me...as a brother in Christ.... a fellow soldier'.

And so too did Charles:

> 'Love, like death, hath all destroyed,
> Rendered all distinctions void;
> Names, and sects, and parties fall;
> Thou, O Christ, art all in all'.

Many other aspects of their subsequent religious thinking can be found in her advice to them. One obvious example is their dislike of Calvinism with its belief that people were pre-ordained for either salvation or damnation. Susanna told them not to confuse God's foreknowledge of how people would respond to the gospel message with God making them behave like that. It was like saying 'that our knowing the sun will rise tomorrow is the cause of its rise'. Calvinism in its most rigid form was 'very shocking and.... inconsistent with the justice and goodness of God'. Similarly their emphasis on the importance of taking regular communion clearly originated in part from her:

> 'There is nothing more proper or effectual for the strengthening and refreshing the mind than the frequent partaking of that blessed ordinance'.

It would be wrong, however, to assume that John always entirely agreed with his mother. Perhaps the most obvious example is on the issue of Christian perfection. Susanna taught her children to 'press after greater degrees of Christian perfection' but felt that, however much a person loved God, he or she was still a prey to human sinfulness: 'We are all by nature corrupt and impure, and the best are but sanctified in part'. This meant no one in practice ever became perfect until after death:

> 'Perfection.... in this life amounts to no more than a perfection of degrees... [and even] the sublimest patch of virtue that ever any reached is unworthy the name of true perfection'.

For her what mattered was not attaining perfection but seeking it:

> *'Be not you discouraged with your own failings, nor.... spend so much time thinking on them. Consider that perfection is thy Saviour's endowment, sincerity is thine. His merits (if relied on by a firm faith joined with your sincere endeavour to obey the whole will of God) will supply thy deficiencies.'*

Charles accepted her approach but John did not. He held that Christians could become perfect if only they had enough faith and this view was to cause much unhelpful dissension among Methodists.

What Susanna consistently provided to her sons was encouragement. When her husband died and she was made homeless, she still fully supported John and Charles leaving for America to become missionaries:

> *'Had I twenty sons I should rejoice that they were all so employed, though I should never see them more'.*

She similarly backed them when they returned to Britain and declined seeking proper positions in the Church in order to launch a religious revival. At first she was disturbed by her eldest son's arguments that they were linking themselves with a religious fanatic by working with George Whitefield, but, when she met Whitefield, she told Samuel she was convinced he was 'one who truly desires the salvation of mankind'. Interestingly, her own faith seems to have undergone a deepening in 1739 through understanding what John and Charles were trying to achieve. The years since her husband's death had been very difficult. She had tried living in the homes first of Emily, then of Samuel, and finally of Patty, but had found their partners difficult to live with. She had, in her own words, 'no taste, no relish left for anything'. Seeing John and Charles made her feel her life had not been wasted and during a communion service in August 1739 she felt a new sense of assurance that 'God had forgiven me all my sins':

> *'When I was almost without hope, when I had forgotten God, yet I then found he had not forgotten me.'*

Both John and Charles wrongly interpreted this as their mother having the same 'heart strangely warmed' experience as themselves rather than her emerging from a state of depression.

Fate still had blows to inflict on Susanna. In November 1739 her eldest son Samuel unexpectedly died. She told Charles:

> *'Your brother was exceeding dear to me in this life, and perhaps I have erred in loving him too well. I once thought it impossible to bear his loss, but none know what they can bear till they are tried'.*

In 1741 she also suffered the loss of her youngest daughter, Kezzy. However, by then Susanna was safely ensconced in the building created by John and Charles as their London base. The years she spent at the Foundery from 1740 to 1742 were Susanna's happiest. She was looked after well and accepted that gratefully: 'In the most literal sense, I have become a little child and want continual succour'. She welcomed the opportunity to regularly see not only John and Charles but also Emily who joined her at the Foundery and three of her other daughters, who were living in or near London (Sukey, Hetty, and, until her death, Kezzy). She witnessed with delight John preaching to thousands on Kensington Common and was proud of the impact he and Charles were having in both London and Bristol. Her only complaint was that some of the Methodists were too obsessed with the state of their faith: 'I have often wished they would talk less of themselves and more of God'.

Remarkably it was her advice that convinced John to officially use lay preachers. While her sons were away, one of their supporters, Thomas Maxfield, began leading worship and Susanna was impressed. John had been turning a blind eye to this (as indeed he was also doing in Bristol where another young man, John Cennick, was preaching), but felt the stage was being reached when he would either have to endorse what was happening or stop it. He asked Susanna's opinion and she said: 'Thomas Maxfield is as much called to preach the Gospel as ever you were'.

In 1742 Susanna's health finally collapsed and she died 'calm and serene' on 30 July surrounded by John and all her surviving daughters. Charles unfortunately had been called away. Just before she lost her speech she told them: 'Children, as soon as I am released, sing a psalm of praise to God'. She was buried in the dissenters' burial ground in Bunhill Fields (opposite the future site of the City Road Chapel) and John wrote of her funeral 'it was one of the most solemn assemblies I ever saw or expect to see this side of eternity'. He gave the funeral address and Charles wrote the verse to be engraved on her stone:

> 'In sure and steadfast hope to rise,
> And claim her mansion in the skies;
> A Christian here her flesh laid down,
> The Cross exchanging for a Crown....'

Her influence lived on not only in what John and Charles were saying but what they were doing. She had told them: 'Jesus when on earth went about doing good. And you must do what good you can'. Both brothers regularly visited prisons. Charles proved a dedicated pastor and John organised schools, orphanages, homes for widows, medical dispensaries, and much more. Most famously he also campaigned against the slave trade.

Susanna's writings were written only for her own contemplation and the benefit of her children, but in a real sense John and Charles gave them public expression through their witness and work. Though one can trace all kinds of other influences on them I suspect both brothers would have acknowledged that Susanna truly was 'the mother of Methodism'. It is fitting therefore that the one document that Susanna did write for publication was a defence of her sons' work. In 1742 she published a tract called 'Some Remarks on a Letter from the Rev. Mr Whitefield' defending their theological position and their actions:

> *'I cannot but observe how signally God hath honoured those two brethren… by calling them forth and enabling them with great power to preach the truth of the gospel as it is in Jesus and by setting his seal to their ministry. And I am persuaded you will join with me in prayer to our Lord. That he would strengthen and bless them more and more and protect them from evil men and evil angels, and that they may be steadfast, immovable, always abounding in the work of the Lord'.*

The inscription at the City Road Chapel that commemorates Susanna's burial in the nearby Bunhill Fields Burial Ground

Acknowledgements

Detail of Susanna from oil on canvas, artist unknown, on front cover and details on page 25 from oil on canvas of John Wesley by Margaret Grose, 1920, (in manner of Nathaniel Hone) and from oil on canvas of Charles Wesley in the manner of Thomas Hudson, c.1740 are copyright Epworth Old Rectory and reproduced with kind permission of the trustees of Epworth Old Rectory. So also are external photos of the Rectory and photos 1 and 4 of the interior. Other interior photos copyright the author.